GERTA O. EGY

MUSHROOM DAYDREAM
Coloring Book

MICROCOSM PUBLISHING
PORTLAND, OR ⬡ CLEVELAND, OH

MUSHROOM DAYDREAM

ISBN 9781648413162
This is Microcosm #752
First published March 19, 2024

This edition © Microcosm Publishing, 2024

For a catalog, write or visit:
Microcosm Publishing
2752 N Williams Ave.
Portland, OR 97227
www.Microcosm.Pub/Mushroom

To join the ranks of high-class stores that feature Microcosm titles, talk to your rep: In the U.S. **COMO** (Atlantic), **ABRAHAM** (Midwest), **BOB BARNETT** (Texas, Oklahoma, Arkansas, Louisiana), **IMPRINT** (Pacific), **TURNAROUND** (UK), **UTP/MANDA** (Canada), **NEWSOUTH** (Australia/New Zealand), **OBSERVATOIRE** (Africa, Middle East, Europe), **Yvonne Chau** (Southeast Asia), **HARPERCOLLINS** (India), **EVEREST/ B.K. Agency** (China), **TIM BURLAND** (Japan/Korea), and **FAIRE** and **EMERALD** in the gift trade.

Did you know that you can buy our books directly from us at sliding scale rates? Support a small, independent publisher and pay less than Amazon's price at **www.Microcosm.Pub**.

Global labor conditions are bad, and our roots in industrial Cleveland in the '70s and '80s made us appreciate the need to treat workers right. Therefore, our books are MADE IN THE USA.

Microcosm Publishing is Portland's most diversified publishing house and distributor with a focus on the colorful, authentic, and empowering. Our books and zines have put your power in your hands since 1996, equipping readers to make positive changes in their lives and in the world around them. Microcosm emphasizes skill-building, showing hidden histories, and fostering creativity through challenging conventional publishing wisdom with books and bookettes about DIY skills, food, bicycling, gender, self-care, and social justice. What was once a distro and record label started by Joe Biel in a drafty bedroom was determined to be *Publishers Weekly*'s fastest-growing publisher of 2022 and has become among the oldest independent publishing houses in Portland, OR, and Cleveland, OH. We are a politically moderate, centrist publisher in a world that has inched to the right for the past 80 years.